PIANO • VOCAL • GUITAR

BILLY JOEL STORM FRONT

Additional editing and transcription by David Rosenthal

ISBN 978-1-4950-2030-8

Visit Hal Leonard Online at
www.halleonard.com

Contact Us:
Hal Leonard
7777 West Bluemound Road
Milwaukee, WI 53213
Email: info@halleonard.com

In Europe contact:
Hal Leonard Europe Limited
Distribution Centre, Newmarket Road
Bury St Edmunds, Suffolk, IP33 3YB
Email: info@halleonardeurope.com

In Australia contact:
Hal Leonard Australia Pty. Ltd.
4 Lentara Court
Cheltenham, Victoria, 3192 Australia
Email: info@halleonard.com.au

CONTENTS

FOREWORD

Storm Front was released in 1989 and entered the Billboard Charts at #1. It was Billy's 11th studio album of original material. Co-produced by Billy and Mick Jones, this was the first album since 1976 without producer Phil Ramone at his side. It was a stormy time in Billy's life on many fronts—changes in the band, lawsuits with former management, turbulent events in America and the world, all of which impacted and influenced the music and lyrics on this album.

These challenges are also represented in the album's iconic artwork. As Billy describes the cover image and concept, "The flag you see on the cover is a hurricane flag, #10 on the Beaufort scale, red with a black square in the middle. It means the worst weather conditions possible. When you see that flag you don't go anywhere. Either you pull your boat out of the water, or you head out to sea and drive into the face of the storm."

The first single from the album was "We Didn't Start The Fire," one of the few songs where Billy wrote the words first. It was a #1 single in many countries around the world, yet remains Billy's least favorite composition musically. However, it's rapid fire lyrics—pulled from worldwide events during Billy's life, starting with his birth in 1949 to his inspiration for the song in 1989—engage people of all ages, and the energy of the song ignites audiences whenever we perform it live.

Having played keyboards in Billy Joel's band since 1993, I have an inside perspective into his music. Accordingly, Billy asked that I review every note of the sheet music in his entire catalog of songs. As a pianist, he entrusted me with the task of correcting and re-transcribing each piece to ensure that the printed music represents each song exactly as it was written and recorded. *Storm Front* is the latest edition in our series of revised songbooks in the Billy Joel catalog, which began with *The Stranger* songbook back in 2008.

The challenge with each folio in Billy's catalog is to find musical ways to combine his piano parts and vocal melodies into playable piano arrangements. First, the signature piano parts were transcribed and notated exactly as Billy played them. The vocal melodies were then transcribed and incorporated into the piano part in a way that preserves the original character of each song.

"Leningrad," a personal favorite of mine, was written about Billy's experiences on his trip to Russia in 1987. He captures the feeling of Russia, not only through the lyrical pictures in the story he tells, but also in the movement and voice leading in his chord changes. The mood for the song is perfectly set up in the intro, which is transcribed here note-for-note.

The simple beauty of "And So it Goes" is instantly notable, but a closer look at Billy's piano voicings reveal brilliant contrasts of dissonances and resolutions, which enhance the tension in the lyric. The exact piano voicings he played in the intro and in both intro reprises are accurately notated here. The vocal melodies are combined into the piano voicings to create a playable part.

Itzhak Perlman was the guest violinist who performed on "The Downeaster Alexa" (although in the liner notes he is credited as "World Famous Incognito Violinist"!). His characteristic parts help create the mood of rising and falling seas and passing sea gulls in this powerful song about the struggles of the Long Island baymen. In this revision of the sheet music, Itzhak's violin parts are now captured in the piano accompaniment that supports the vocal melodies, and his solo is integrated into the piano part.

On "State of Grace," I combined the cathedral organ part and the high-octaves piano part to capture as much of the character of this section as possible when playing it only on piano. The melody of the guitar solo is combined into the piano part to create a playable part.

The energetic rocker "I Go to Extremes" fades out on the recording, so I included an optional ending that is the same as we perform it live.

The signature sax lines in "When in Rome" are included and woven into the piano part, as is the guitar solo in "Shameless."

All of the songs in this collection received the same astute attention to detail. The result is sheet music that is both accurate and enjoyable to play, and that remains true to the original performances.

Billy and I are pleased to present the revised and now accurate sheet music to the timeless album *Storm Front*.

Enjoy,

David Rosenthal
September 2017

THAT'S NOT HER STYLE

Words and Music by
BILLY JOEL

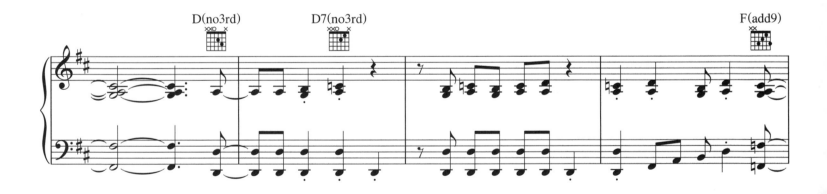

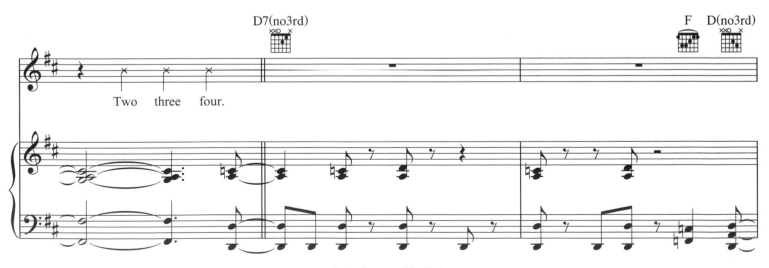

Two three four.

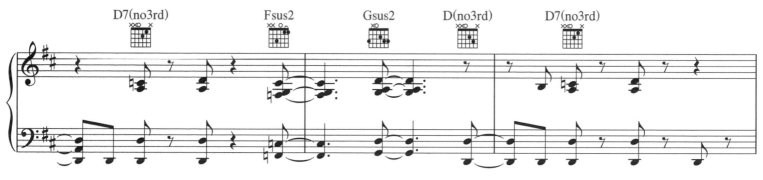

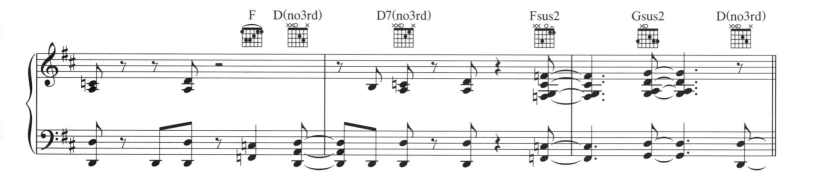

Some peo - ple think that she's one of those mink-coat - ed la - dies.
The pa - pers say __ she was seen in L. A. __ with a stran - ger.

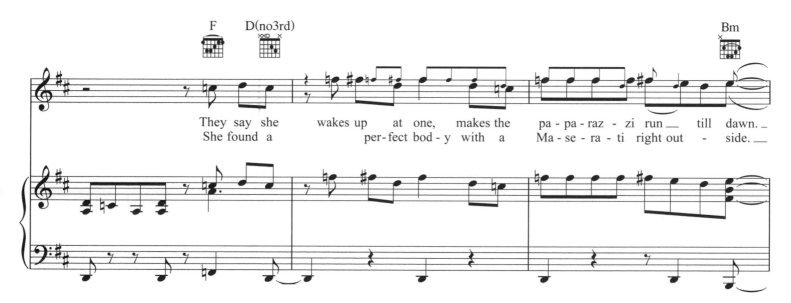

They say she wakes up at one, makes the pa - pa - raz - zi run __ till dawn. __
She found a per - fect bod - y with a Ma - se - ra - ti right out - side. __

You know it's not her style _____ I can tell ____ you, 'cause I'm her man. _

It's not that she's nev -

- er done some-thing cra - zy, __ done some-thing wild. _____

It's just that she's bet - ter at do - ing what-ev - er suits __ her style; _

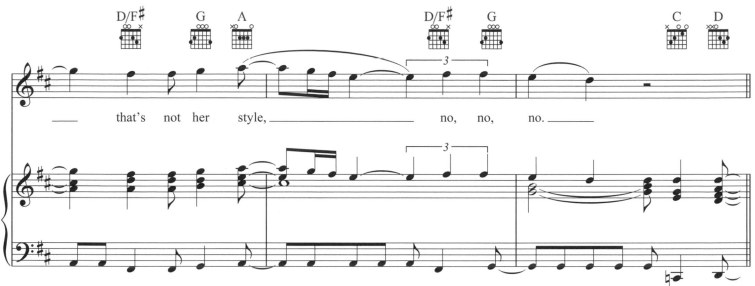

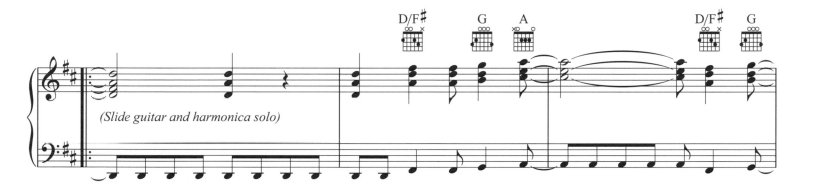

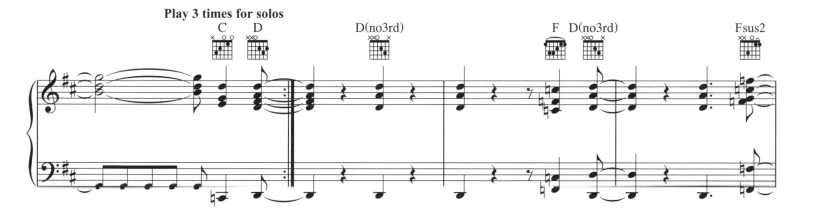

It's just not her style _____ I can tell ___ you, 'cause I am her ___

man. That's not her style. _

_____ That's not her style. _

Repeat with ad libs. and Fade

(Vocal ad lib.)

WE DIDN'T START THE FIRE

Words and Music by
BILLY JOEL

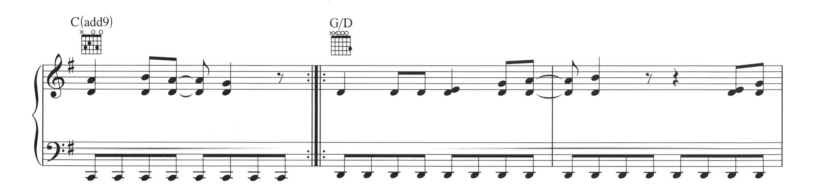

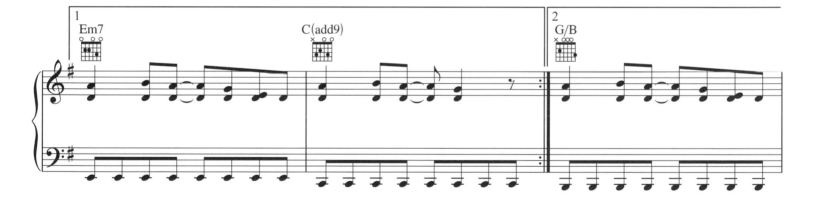

Har - ry Tru - man, Dor - is Day, Red Chi - na, John - nie Ray,

South Pa-cif-ic, Wal-ter Win-chell, Joe Di-Mag-gi-o. Joe Mc-Car-thy, Rich-ard Nix-on,

Stu-de-bak-er, tel-e-vi-sion, North Ko-re-a, South Ko-re-a, Mar-i-lyn Mon-roe.

Ro-sen-bergs, H - Bomb, Sug-ar Ray, Pan-mun-jom,
Bud-dy Hol-ly, Ben Hur, Space Mon-key, Ma-fi-a,

G/B

C(add9)

-re.   No, we did- n't light __ it, but we tried to fight __ it.

G

Dsus

Jo - seph Sta - lin,   Ma - len - kov,   Nas - ser and Pro - kof - i - ev,

Hem - ing - way,   Eich - mann,   Stran - ger In A Strange Land.

Em(add4)

C

G

Rock - e - fel - ler, Cam - pa - nel - la,   Com - mu - nist Bloc.   Roy __ Cohn, Juan Pe - rón,

Dy - lan, Ber - lin,   Bay of Pigs In - va - sion.   Law-rence of A - ra - bi - a,

Dsus

Em(add4)

C

Tos - ca - ni - ni, Da - cron.   Dien Bien Phu Falls,   Rock A - round the Clock.

Brit - ish Bea - tle - ma - ni - a.   Ole Miss, John Glenn,   Lis - ton beats Pat - ter - son.

Ein - stein, James Dean, Brook-lyn's got a win-ning team, Dav - y Crock- ett, Pet - er Pan,
Pope Paul, Mal-colm X, Brit - ish pol - i - ti - cian sex, J. F. K. blown a - way,

El - vis Pres - ley, Dis - ney - land. Bar - dot, Bu - da - pest, Al - a - bam - a, Khru - shchev,

Prin - cess Grace, Pey - ton Place, Trou - ble in the Su - ez. We did - n't start the fi -

- re. It was al - ways burn - ing since the world's been turn - ing.

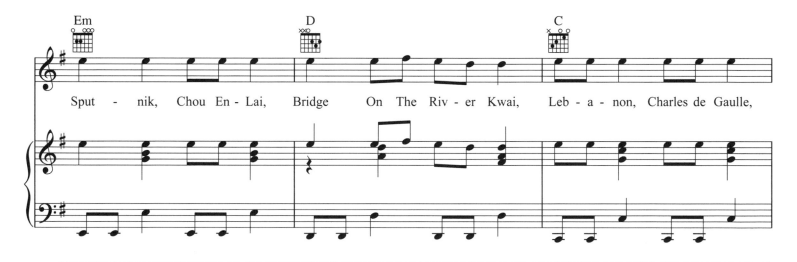

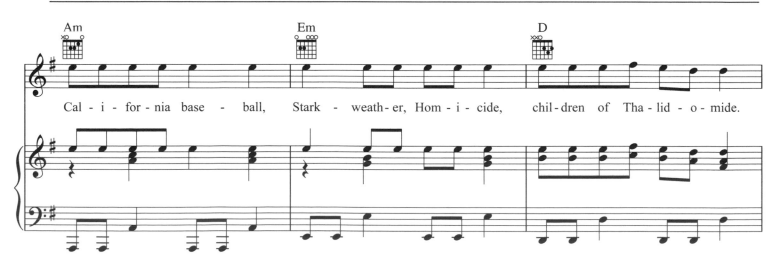

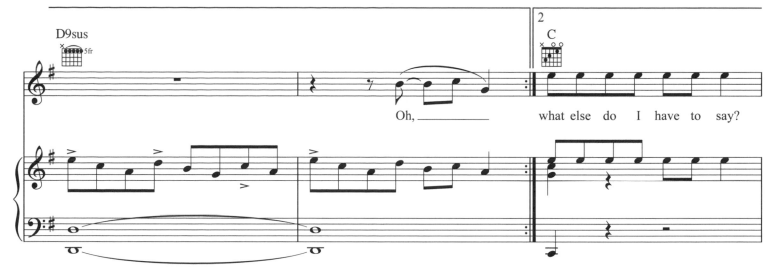

Oh, _____ what else do I have to say?

We did - n't start the fi - re. It was al - ways burn - ing since the

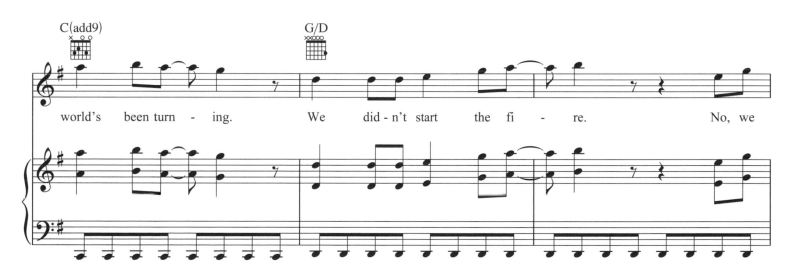

world's been turn - ing. We did - n't start the fi - re. No, we

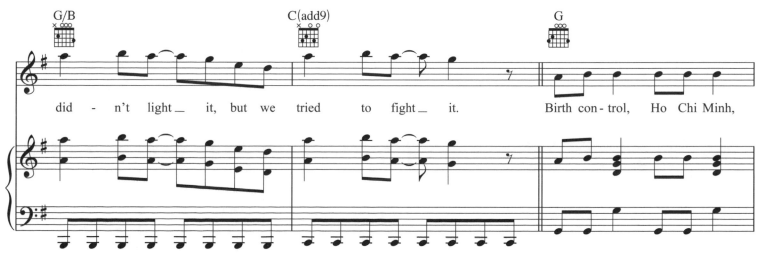

did - n't light __ it, but we tried to fight __ it. Birth con - trol, Ho Chi Minh,

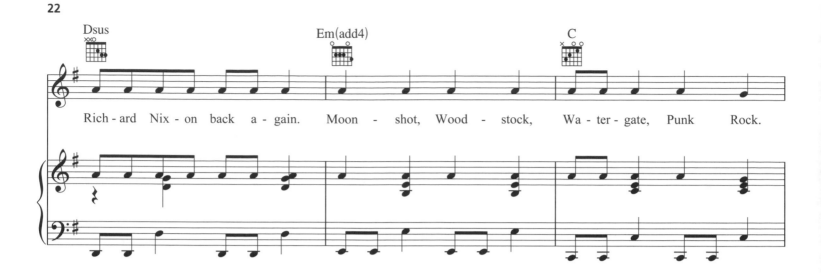

Rich - ard Nix - on back a - gain. Moon - shot, Wood - stock, Wa - ter - gate, Punk Rock.

Be - gin, Rea - gan, Pal - es - tine, Ter - ror on the air - line. Ay - a - tol - lah's in I - ran,

Rus - sians in Af - ghan - i - stan. Wheel of For - tune, Sal - ly Ride, Heav - y Met - al, Su - i - cide,

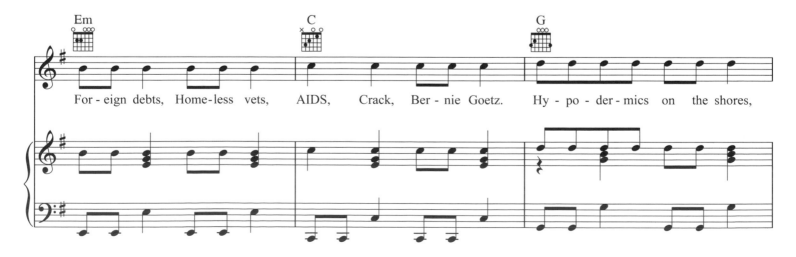

For - eign debts, Home - less vets, AIDS, Crack, Ber - nie Goetz. Hy - po - der - mics on the shores,

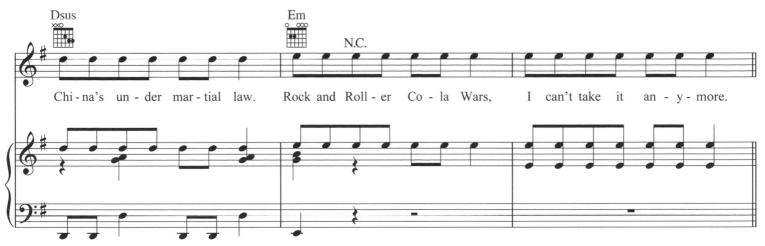

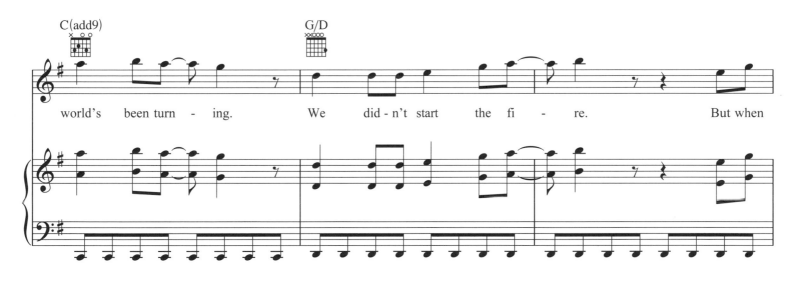

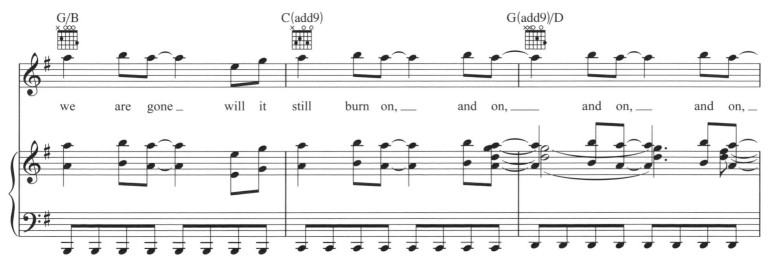

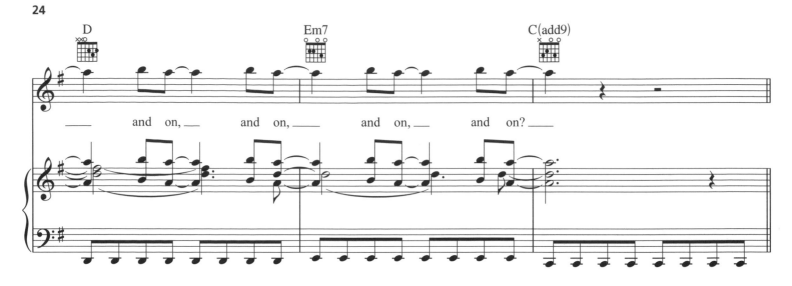

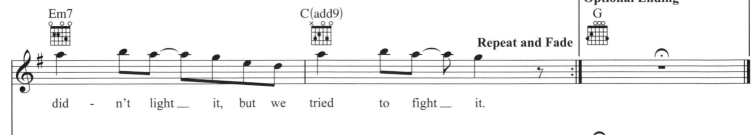

THE DOWNEASTER "ALEXA"

Words and Music by
BILLY JOEL

Not too fast, with a half time feel

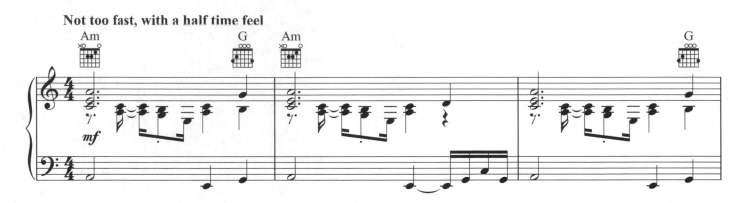

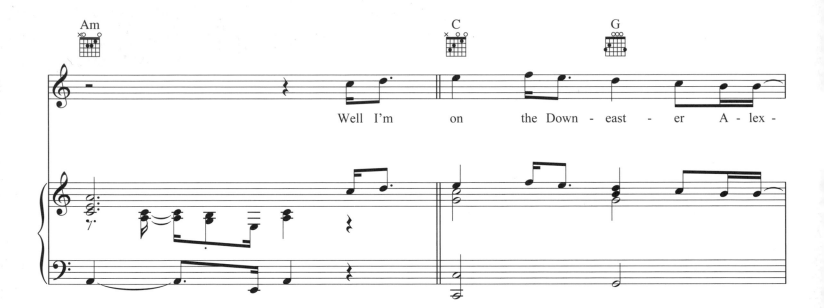

Well I'm on the Down - east - er A - lex -

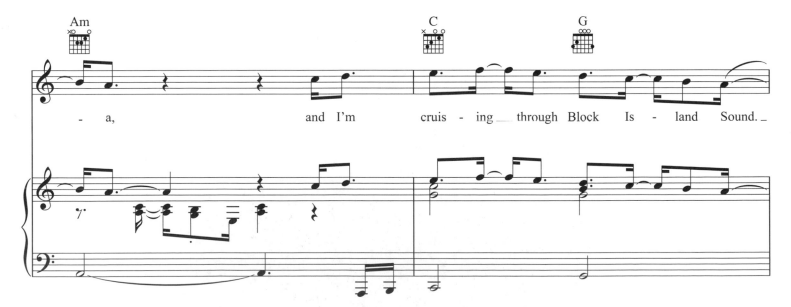

- a, and I'm cruis - ing through Block Is - land Sound.

28

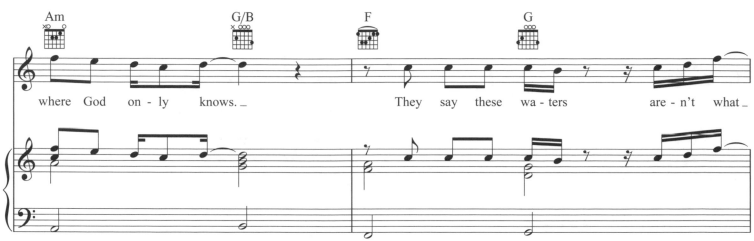

where God on-ly knows. ___ They say these wa-ters are-n't what ___

___ they used to be. ___ But I've got peo-ple back ___ on land ___

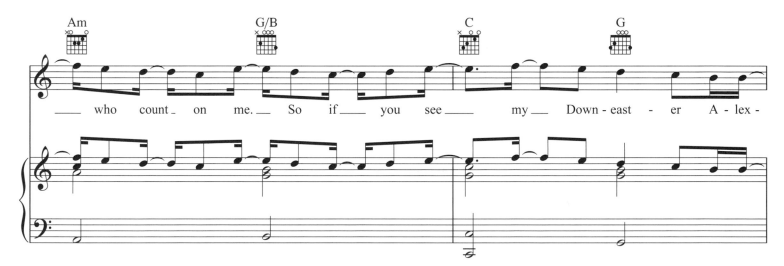

___ who count ___ on me. ___ So if ___ you see ___ my ___ Down-east-er A-lex-

- a, and if you work with the rod ___ and ___ the reel, ___

tell my wife I ___ am troll - ing ___ At - lan -

- tis, and I still have ___ my hands on the wheel. ___

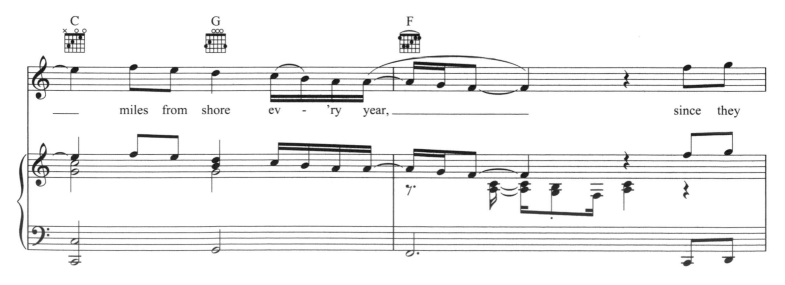

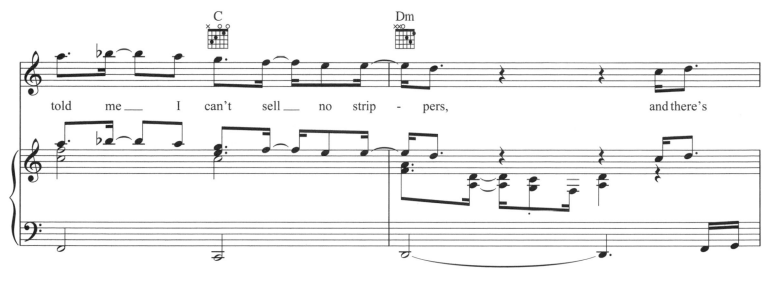

told me ___ I can't sell ___ no strip - pers, and there's

no luck ___ in sword fish-ing here. ___ I was a bay - man like my

fa - ther was ___ be - fore. ___ Can't make a liv - ing as a bay-

- man an - y - more. ___ There ain't much fu - ture for ___ a man ___

who works the sea. But there ain't no is - land left for is -

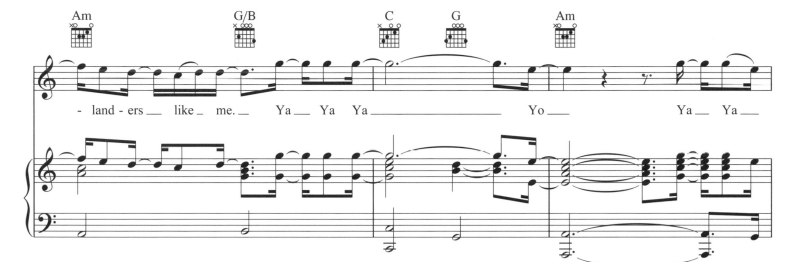

- land-ers like me. Ya Ya Ya Yo Ya Ya

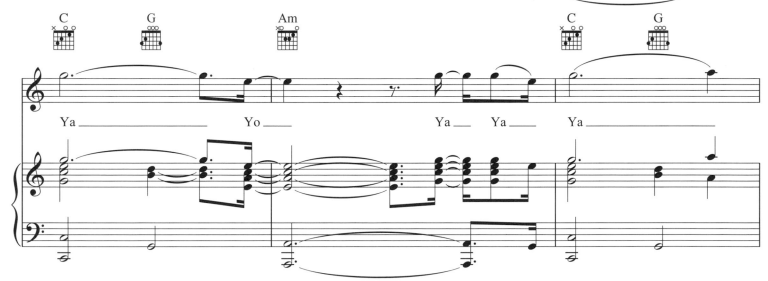

Ya Yo Ya Ya Ya

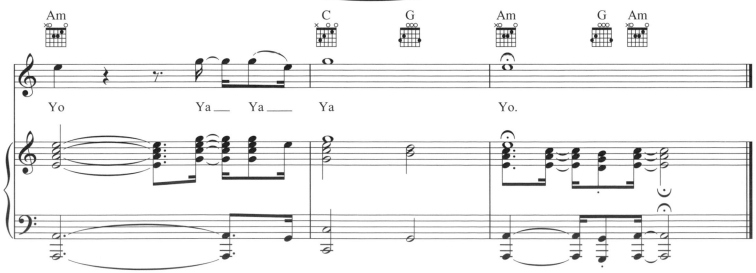

Yo Ya Ya Ya Yo.

Music June 23 89
Lyrics July 5 89

I GO TO EXTREMES

Call me a joker, call me a fool
Right at this moment I'm totally cool
Clear as a crystal, sharp as a knife
I feel like I'm in the prime of my life
Sometimes it feels like I'm going too fast
I don't how ~~long~~ long this feeling will last
Maybe ~~it's only tonight~~ stay with me just for tonight

* chorus
Darling I don't know why I go to extremes
Too high or too low there ain't no in-betweens
You know ~~Right now~~ I can't be denied
Why am I so satisfied
Darlin' I don't know why I go to extremes

Sometimes I'm tired, sometimes I'm shot
Sometimes I don't know how much more I've got
Maybe I'm headed over the hill
Maybe I've set myself up for the kill
Tell me how much do you think you can take
Until the heart in you is starting to break

* chorus
~~Out of the~~
Darling I don't know why I ~~got~~ to extremes
~~Out of the darkness, into the light~~
Too high or too low, there ain't no in-betweens
After I've tried and I've tried
Why am I dissatisfied
Darling I ~~don't~~ know why I go to extremes

~~I've gone as far as I can~~
~~You know this had~~ on

~~Out~~ Out of the darkness, into the light
leaving the scene of the crime
Either I'm wrong, or I'm perfectly right every time
Sometimes I lie awake, night after night
Coming apart at the seams
Eager to please, ~~spoiling~~ ready to fight
Why do I go to extremes

~~You know~~ ~~You know~~ You know how far I can fall
~~that much I already~~ know

And when I rise and I fall

After I've gone through it all
You know how far I can fall
~~Darlin~~ I don't know why I go to extremes

I GO TO EXTREMES

Words and Music by
BILLY JOEL

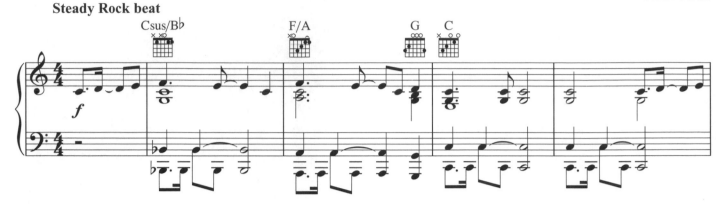

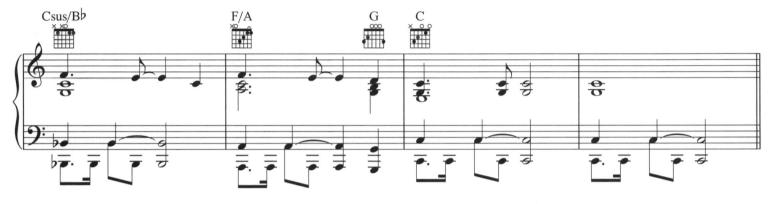

Call me _ a jo-ker, call me _ a fool. Right at _ this mo-ment _ I'm

Some-times _ I'm tired, some-times _ I'm shot. Some-times _ I don't know how

to - tal - ly cool. Clear as _ a crys - tal, sharp as _ a knife,

much more I've got. May-be _ I'm head-ed o - ver _ the hill,

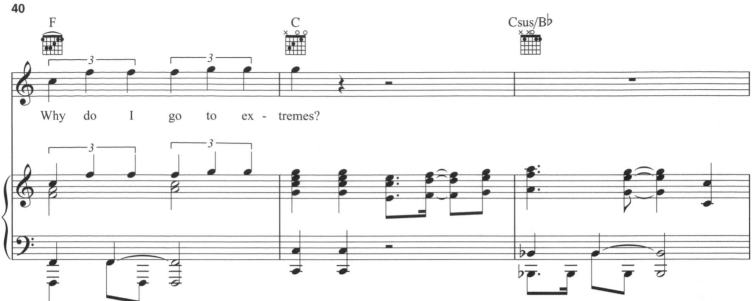

Why do I go to ex - tremes?

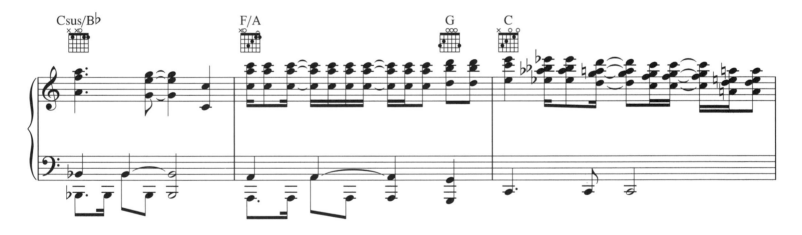

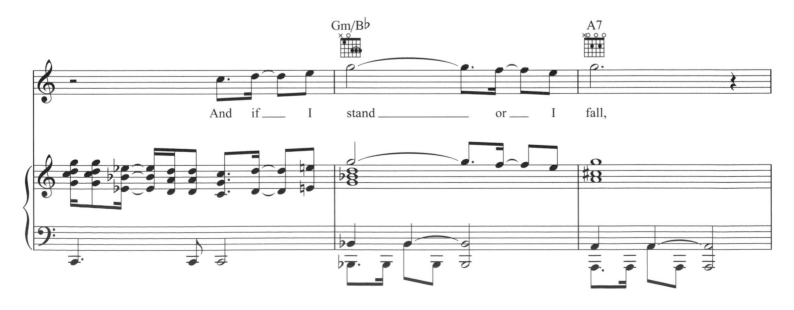

And if ___ I stand _____ or ___ I fall,

SHAMELESS

Words and Music by
BILLY JOEL

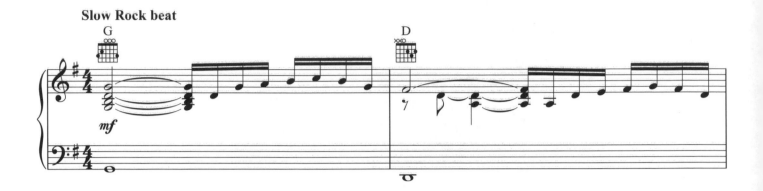

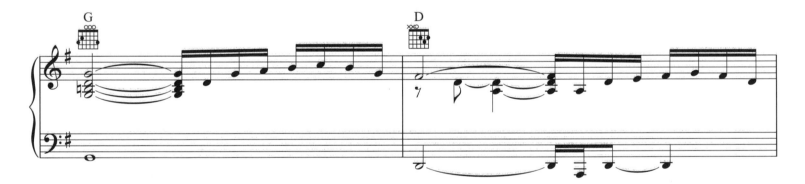

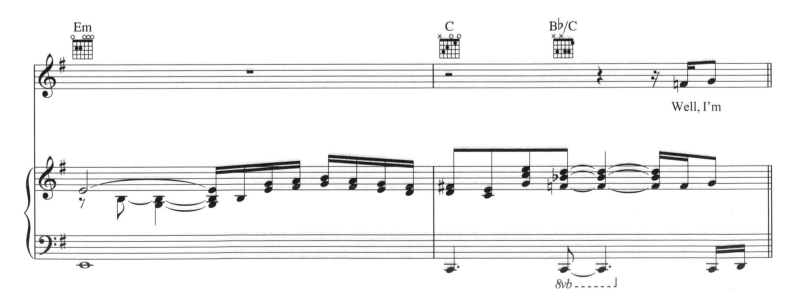

Well, I'm

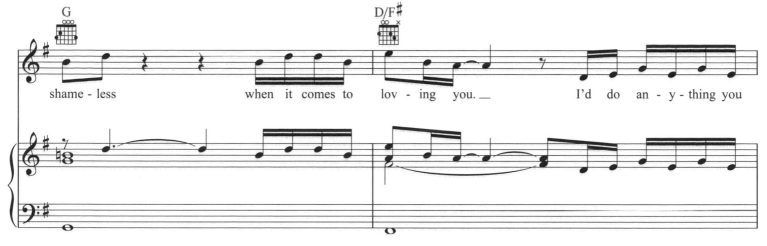

shame - less   when it comes to lov - ing you. __   I'd do an - y - thing you

want me to.   I'd do an - y - thing at all. _____   And I'm

stand - ing   here for all the world to see. _____ Ah, __ there ain't that much

left of me   that has ver - y far to fall. _____   You know __

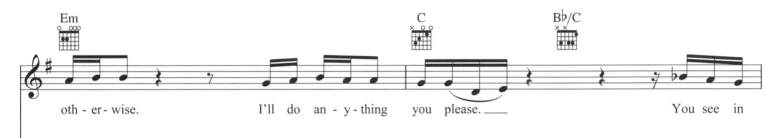

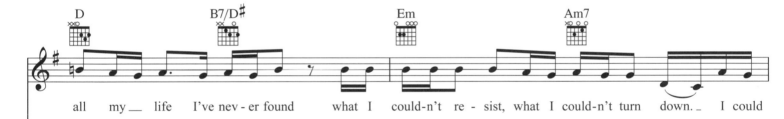

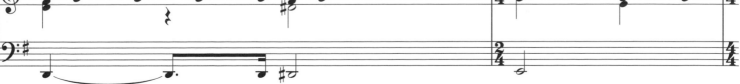

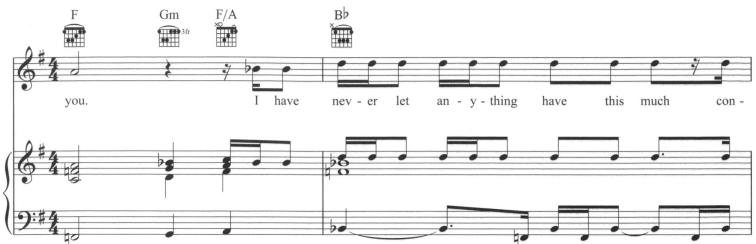

you. I have nev-er let an-y-thing have this much con-

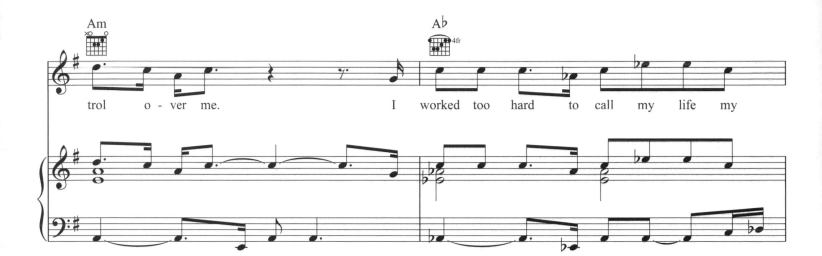

trol o-ver me. I worked too hard to call my life my

own. Well, I made my-self a world and it worked so

per-fect-ly. But it's your world now, I can't re-fuse.

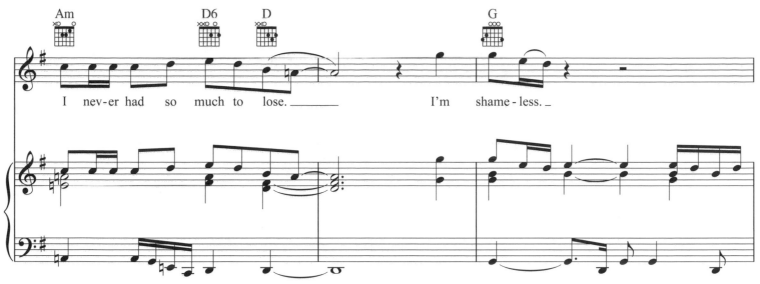

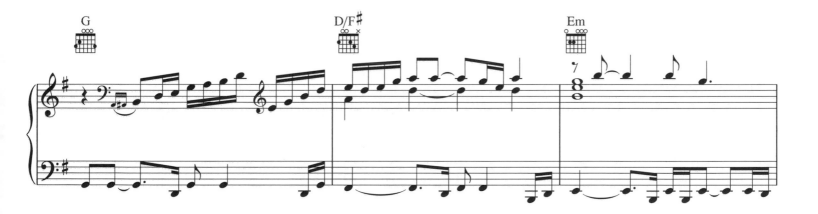

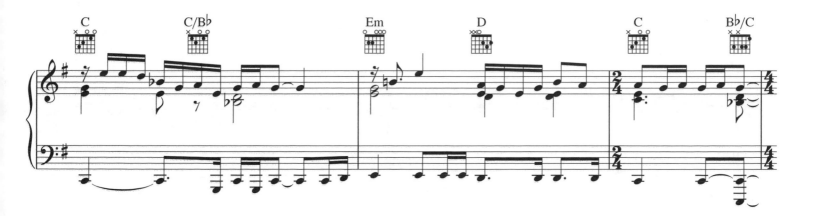

You know it should be eas - y for a man who's strong ___ to

say he's sor - ry or ad - mit when he's wrong. ___ I've nev - er lost an - y - thing I ev - er missed, but

I've nev - er been in love ___ like this. It's out of my hands. ___ I'm

shame - less. ___
shame - less. ___ I don't have the pow - er now. ___ But I don't want it
(Vocal ad lib.)

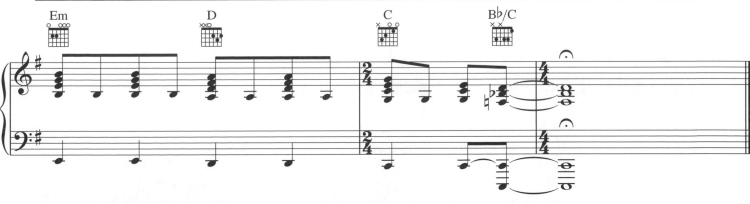

Dec 5 · 88

Storm Front

Safe at harbor, everything is easy
East off ~~~~ to starboard daylight comes up fast
I am restless for the open water
Red flags are flying from the Coast Guard mast
They told me to stay, I heard all the information
I motored away and steered straight ahead
Though the weatherman said
[chorus]
There's a storm front coming [mood indigo]
White water running and the pressure is low
Storm front coming [mood indigo]
Small craft warnings on the radio

I've been sailing long years on this ocean
Man gets lonesome that much time at sea
Still I'm ~~longing~~ for the ~~~~ Big Blue Water
For that power steaming under me
The ~~morning~~ was gray, but I had the motivation
I drifted away and ~~~~ cruised into more
Heavy weather offshore
[chorus]

I've got a woman, my life should be easy
Most men hunger for the life I lead
Still I'm restless for the open water
Though she gives me everything I need all calm on the ~~
And ~~~~ I'd done my navigation
I drove her away
But I should have known
To ~~keep~~ tied up at home
[chorus]

One got a you picked a Real Bad Time
Low pressure system ~~~~ and a tropical gale
It ~~~~ We've got a ~~~~ on the Beaufort scale
We got cumulo nimbus

We got a low pressure system + a northeast breeze
We've got a falling barometer and rising seas
We've got the cumulo nimbus and a ~~~~ gale
We've got a ~~~~ blowing on the Beaufort scale
storm front

One fine morning

We've got a low pressure system
and a northeast breeze
We've got a falling barometer
and rising seas
We've got the cumulo nimbus and a possible gale
We've got a storm front blowing on the Beaufort scale

Leningrad 31 March 89

Viktor was born in the Spring of '44
And never saw his father anymore
A child of sacrifice, a child of war
Another son who never had a father after Leningrad

Went off to school and learned to serve the state
Followed the rules and drank his vodka straight
The only way to live was to drown the hate
A Russian life was very sad
And such was life in Leningrad

"I was born in '49
A cold war kid in McCarthy time
Stop 'em at the 38th Parallel
Blast those yellow Reds to hell, And cold war kids
American kids were hard to kill
Under their desk in an Air raid drill
Haven't they heard we won the war
What do they keep on fighting for?..."
Viktor was sent to some Red Army town, served out his time
They couldn't keep a man like Viktor down, he left
became a circus clown
The greatest happiness he'd ever found
Was making children glad
And children lived in Leningrad

"But children lived in Levittown
And hid in shelters underground, 'til Kruschev turned his
Before they turned their ships around
And tore the Cuban missiles down, then Robert, like his brother John
And Martin Luther King were gone
And I watched my friends go off to war
What do they keep on fighting for? ..."

And so my child and I came to this place
To meet him eye to eye and face to face we embraced
He made my daughter laugh then we embraced
We never knew what friends we had
Until we came to Leningrad

STORM FRONT

Words and Music by
BILLY JOEL

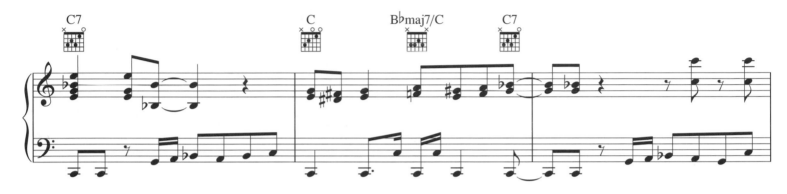

Safe at har -
I've been sail -

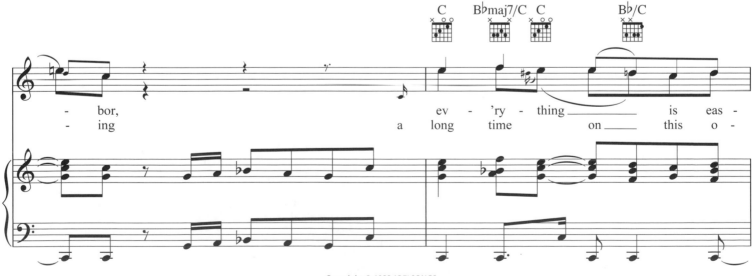

- bor,   ev - 'ry - thing _____ is eas -
- ing   a   long   time   on _____ this o -

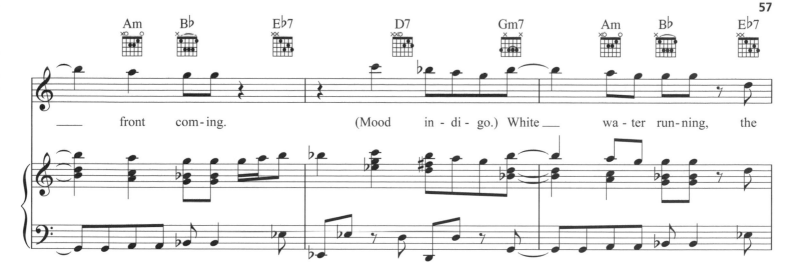

front com-ing. (Mood in-di-go.) White __ wa-ter run-ning, the

pres-sure is low. __ Storm front com-ing. (Mood in-di-go.)

Small craft warn-ing on the ra - di - o. __ Small craft warn-ing on the

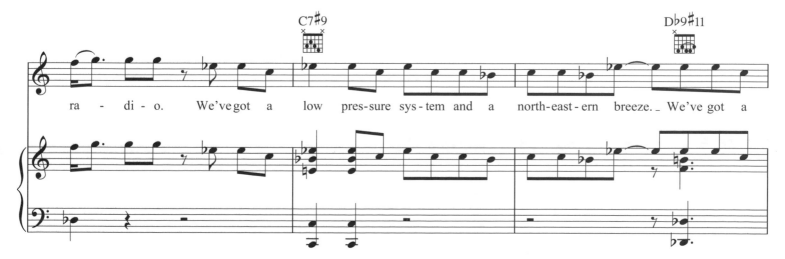

ra - di - o. We've got a low pres-sure sys-tem and a north-east-ern breeze. __ We've got a

fall - ing ba - rom - e - ter and ris - ing seas. __ We've got the cu - mu - lo - nim - bus and a

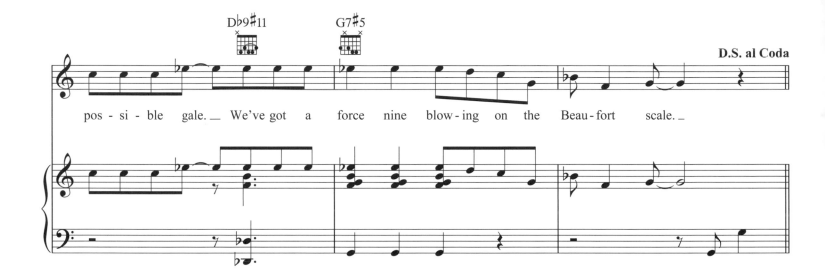

pos - si - ble gale. __ We've got a force nine blow - ing on the Beau - fort scale. __

D.S. al Coda

Small craft warn - ing on the ra - di - o. __

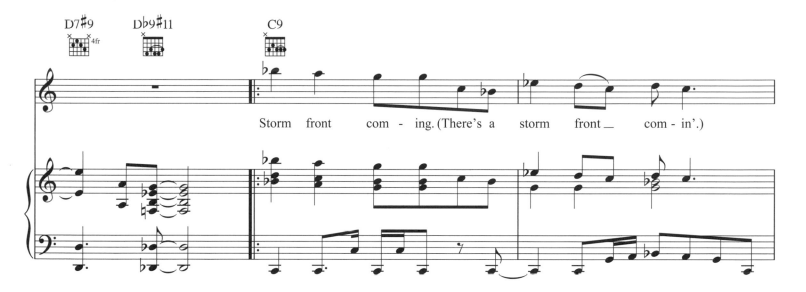

LENINGRAD

Words and Music by
BILLY JOEL

Slow Ballad

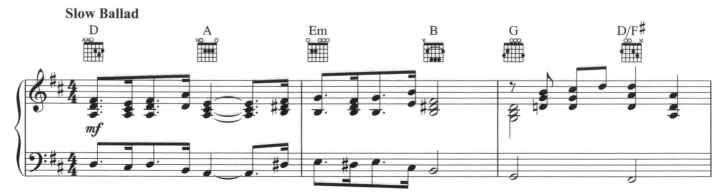

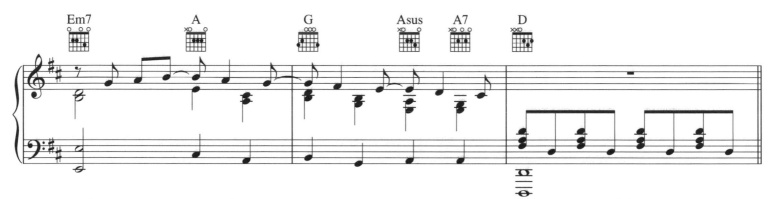

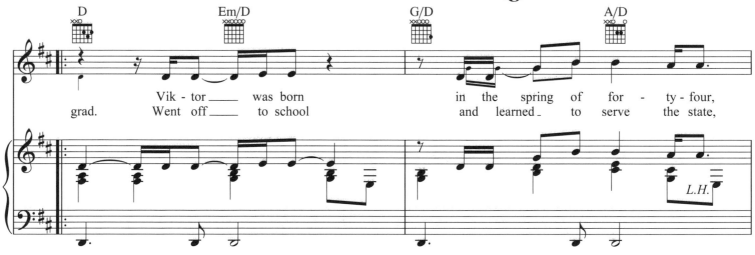

Vik - tor ___ was born in the spring of for - ty - four,
grad. Went off ___ to school and learned ___ to serve the state,

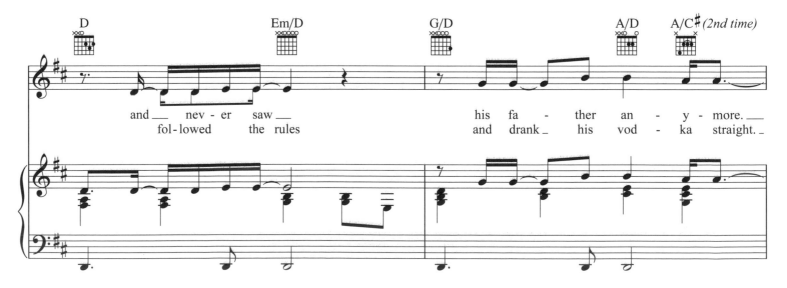

and ___ nev - er saw ___ his fa - ther an - y - more.
fol - lowed the rules and drank ___ his vod - ka straight.

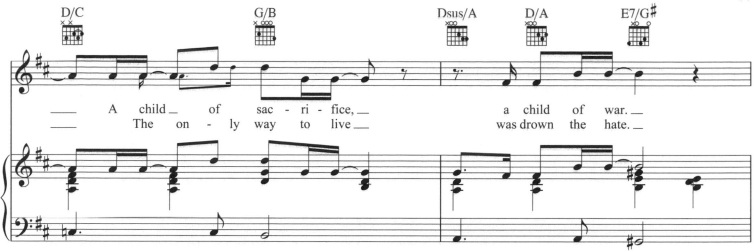

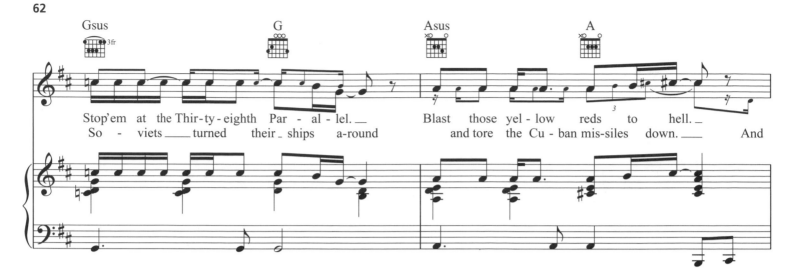

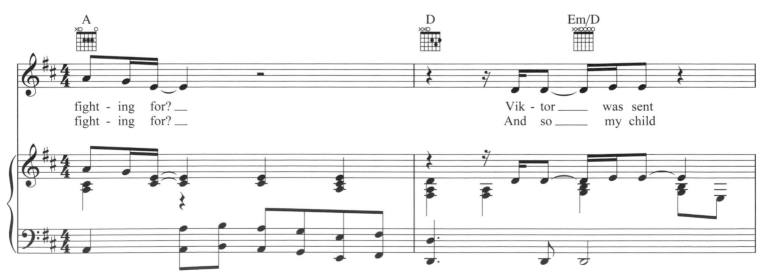

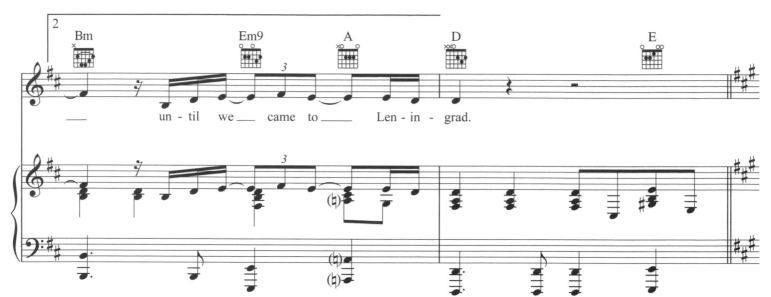

un - til we __ came to __ Len - in - grad.

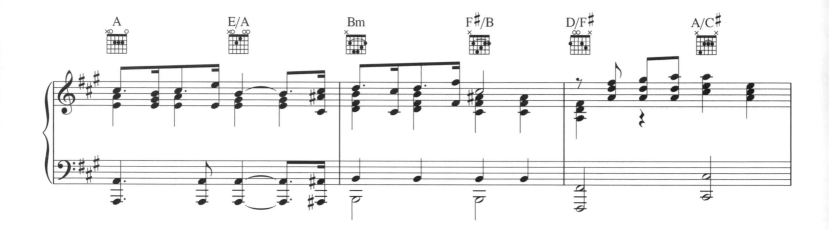

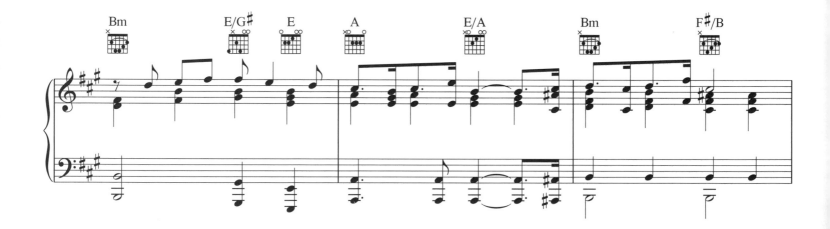

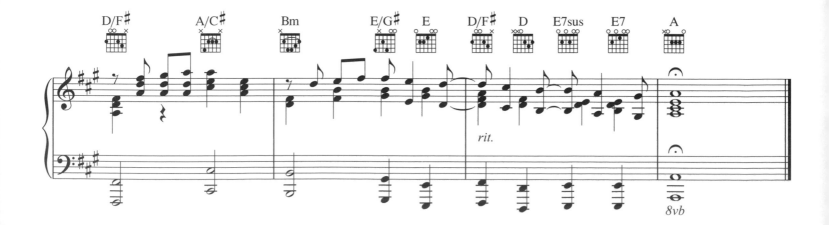

rit.

8vb

STATE OF GRACE

Words and Music by
BILLY JOEL

Moderate Rock

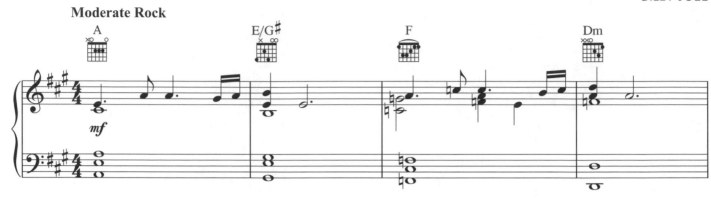

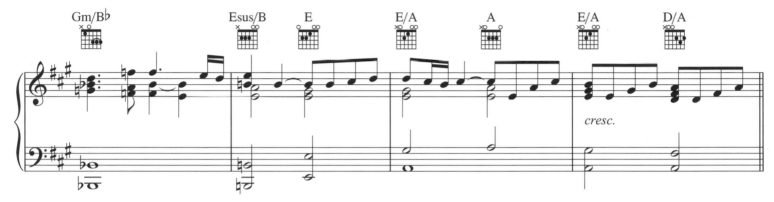

There you go, ___ slip-ping a - way ___ in-to a state of grace. ___
Here I am, ___ try-ing to keep ___ you in my line of sight. ___

I know the look ___ that comes a - cross your face. It's so fa - mil - iar to me. ___
I'm nev - er cer - tain that you read me right. ___ Some-times you don't ___ want to see. ___

67

there you go, __ slip-ping a-way __ in-to a state of grace.
Here I am, __ talk-in' while you __ don't hear a word I say. __

Grant-ed, this world __ is not a per-fect place. __ Still, it's the world that I'm in. __
Know-ing you're watch - ing me from far a - way. __ Some-where that I've __ nev-er been.

Don't you

see, you lived a dif - f'rent life than me. It don't mean you

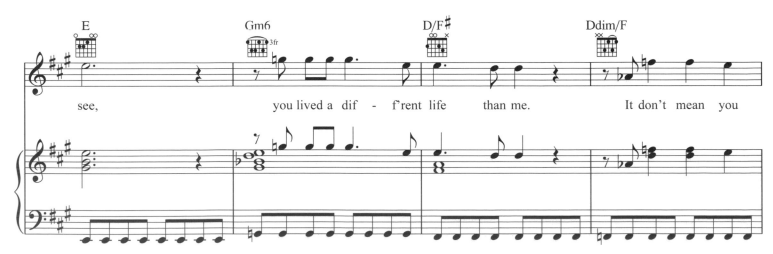

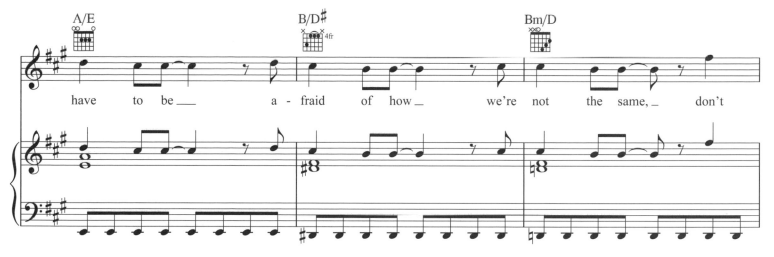

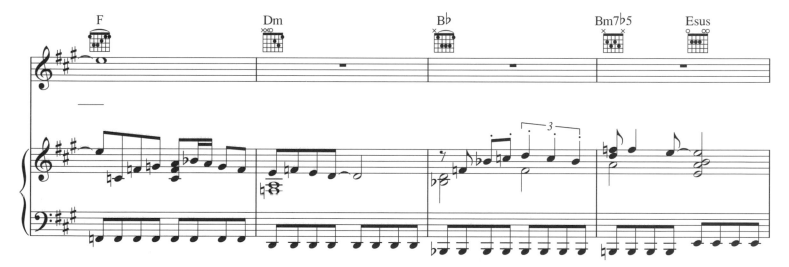

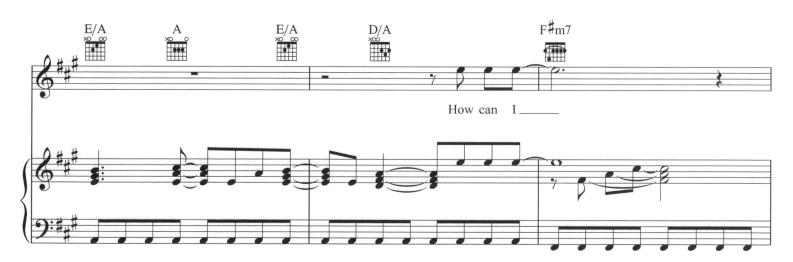

get you to stay __ where you are, _____ keep you from go - ing too far? _____

_____ Hold-ing you here __ is so hard to do. __ I'm

los - ing you. _____

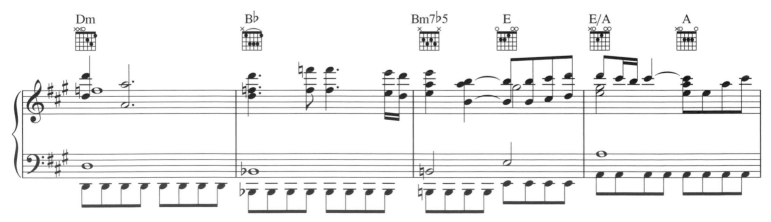

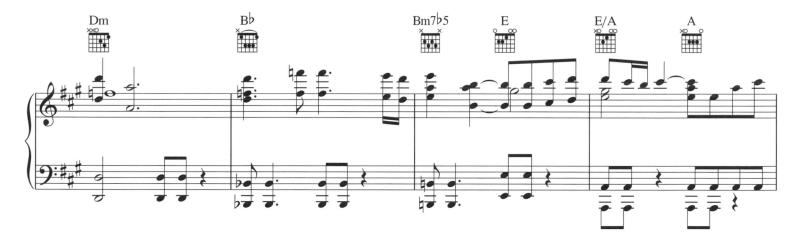

There you go, ____ slip-ping a-way __ in-to a
There you go, _____ slip-ping a-way, __

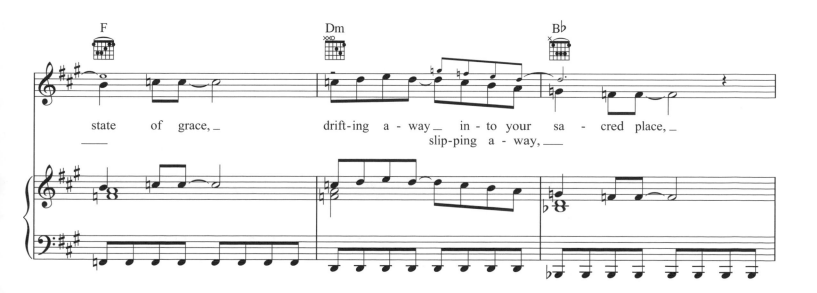

state of grace, __ drift-ing a-way __ in-to your sa - cred place, __
____ slip-ping a - way, ____

WHEN IN ROME

Words and Music by
BILLY JOEL

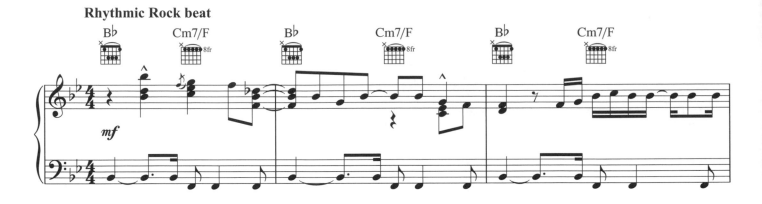

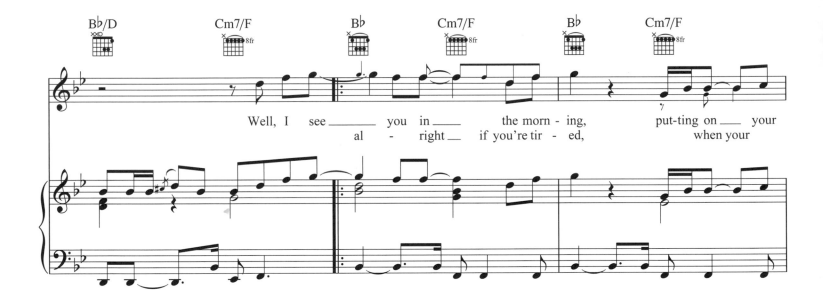

Well, I see _____ you in _____ the morn - ing, put-ting on _____ your
al - right _____ if you're tir - ed, when your

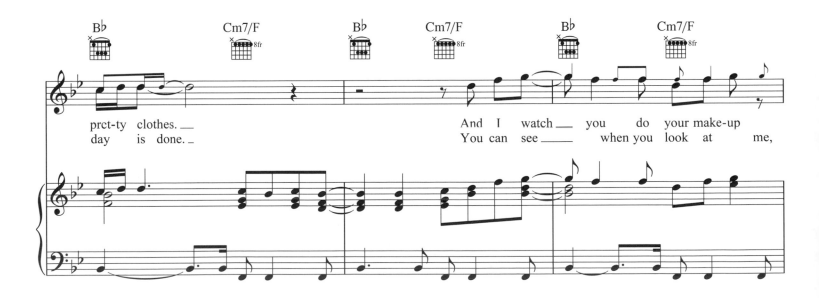

prct-ty clothes. _____ And I watch _____ you do your make-up
day is done. _____ You can see _____ when you look at me,

dar - ling, all you've got to be ___ is you. ___
all it's gon - na be is me ___ and you. ___

When in ___ Rome, ___ do as the Ro - mans do. ___
When in ___ Rome, ___ do as the Ro - mans do. ___

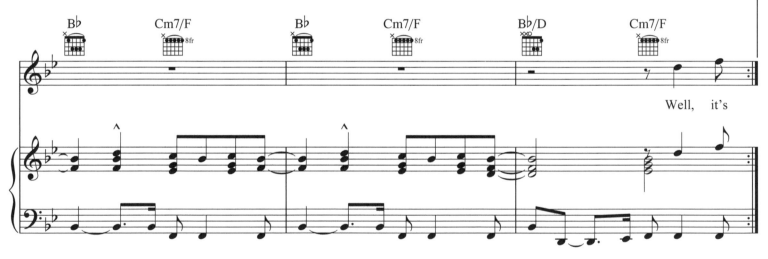

Well, it's

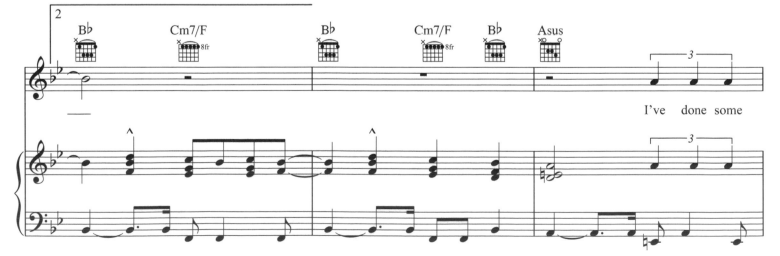

I've done some

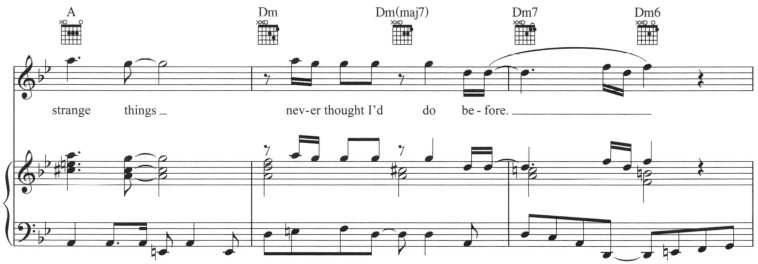

strange things ___ nev-er thought I'd do be - fore. _____

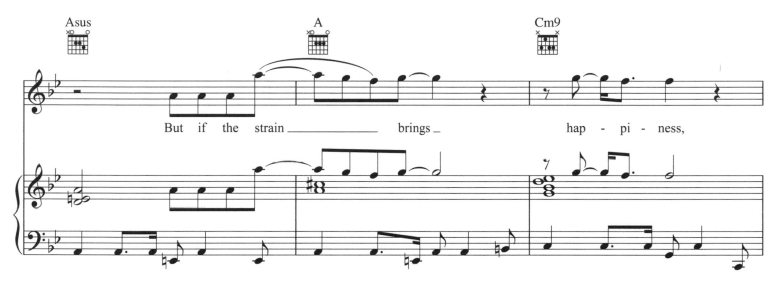

But if the strain _____ brings ___ hap - pi - ness,

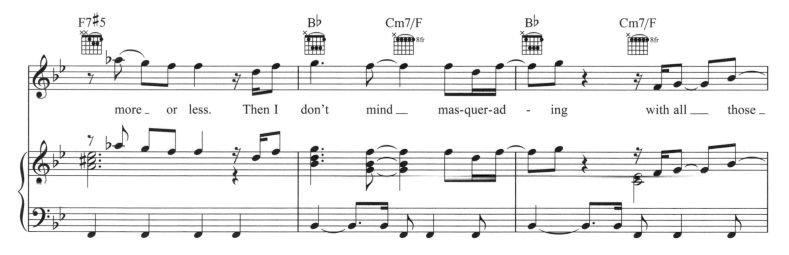

more ___ or less. Then I don't mind ___ mas-quer-ad - ing with all ___ those ___

___ oth-er fools. I don't mind the games ___ I'm play-

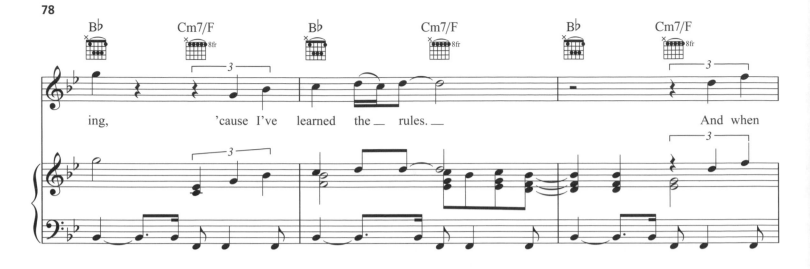

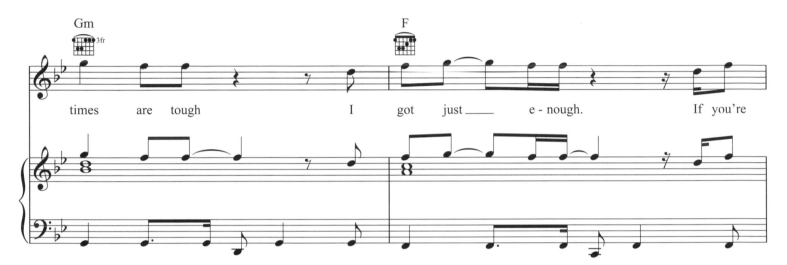

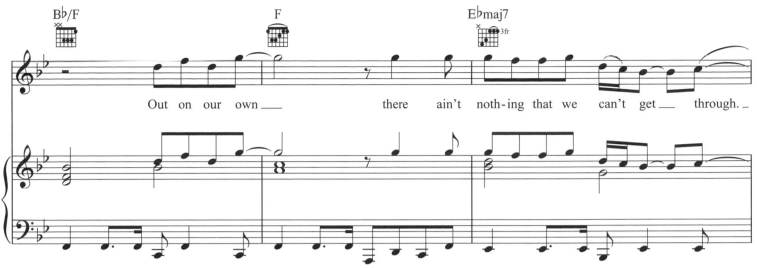

Out on our own ___ there ain't noth-ing that we can't get ___ through. ___

When in ___ Rome, ___ do as the Ro - mans do. ___

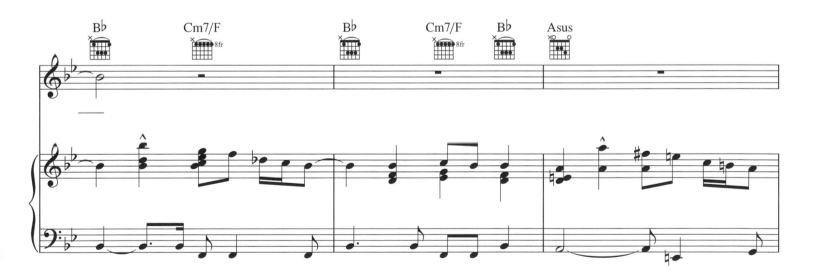

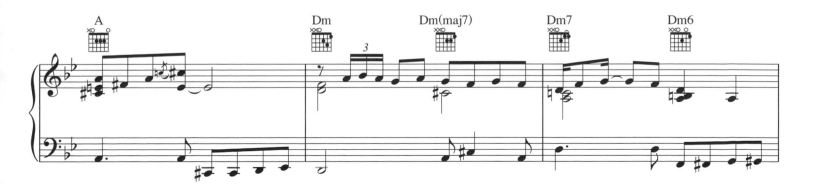

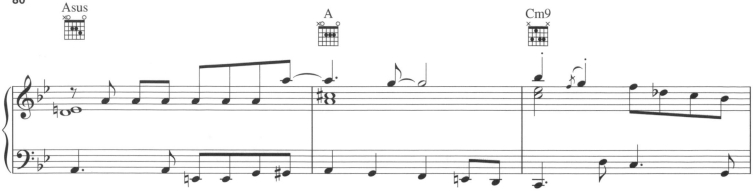

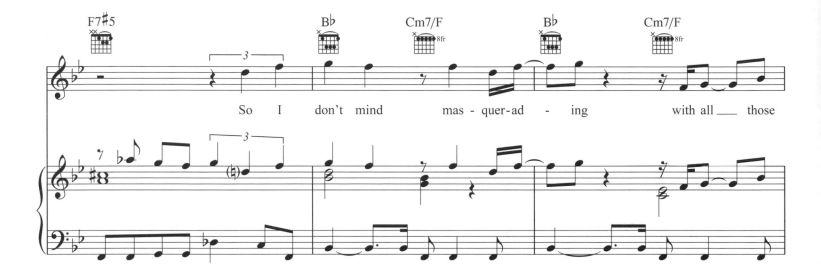

So I don't mind mas-quer-ad - ing with all ___ those

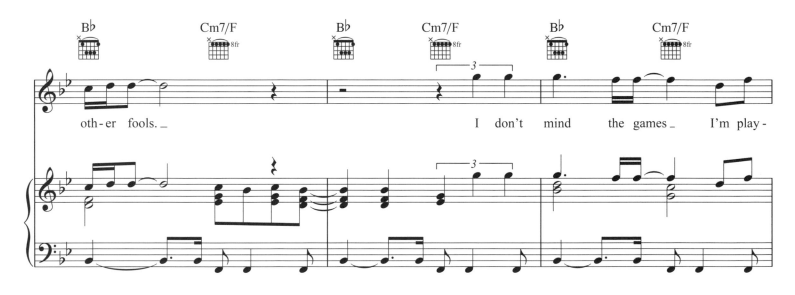

oth-er fools. ___ I don't mind the games ___ I'm play-

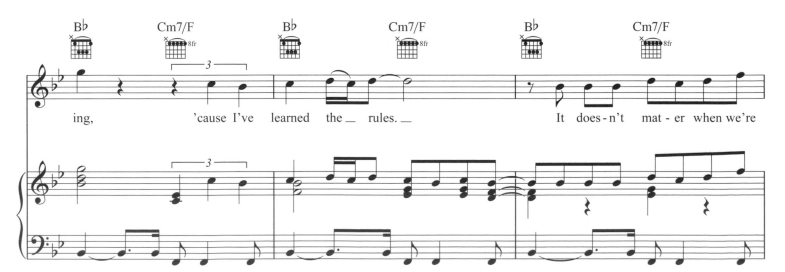

ing, 'cause I've learned the ___ rules. ___ It does-n't mat-er when we're

home _____ all a-lone. All we've got to be is me _____ and you. _____

_____ Out on our own _____ there ain't

noth-ing we can't get through. _____ When in _____ Rome, _____

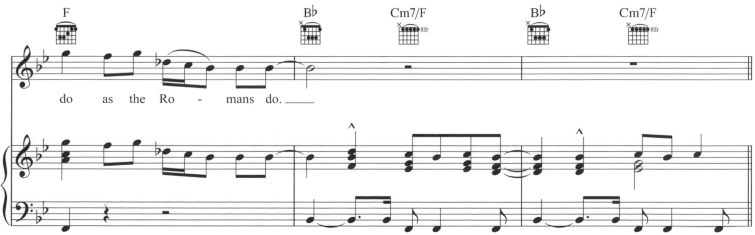

do as the Ro - mans do. _____

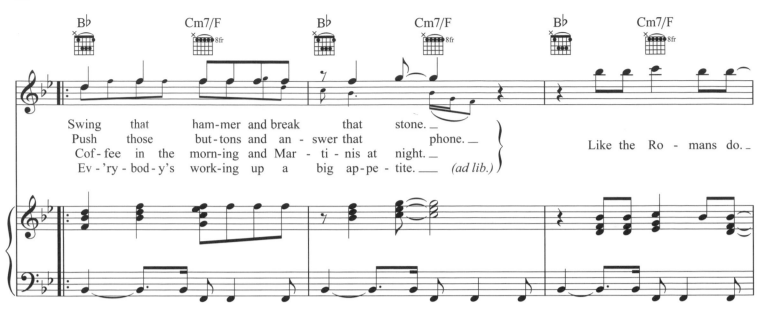

Swing that ham-mer and break that stone. _
Push those but-tons and an - swer that phone. _
Cof - fee in the morn-ing and Mar - ti - nis at night. _
Ev - 'ry - bod - y's work-ing up a big ap-pe - tite. ___ *(ad lib.)*

Like the Ro - mans do. _

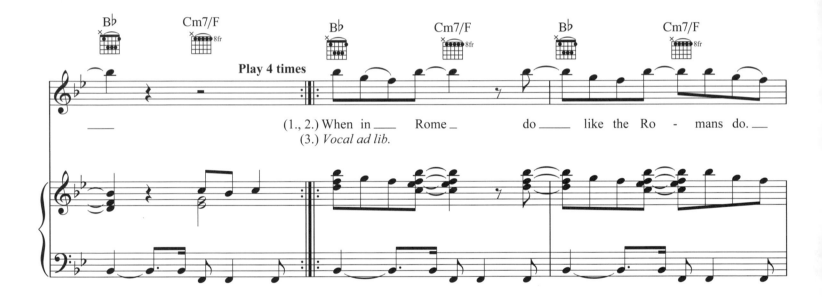

Play 4 times

(1., 2.) When in ___ Rome _ do ___ like the Ro - mans do. _
(3.) *Vocal ad lib.*

1, 2

Like the Ro - mans do. ___

3

Like the Ro - mans do. ___

And So It Goes

In every heart there is a room
A sanctuary safe and strong
To heal the wounds from lovers past
Until a new one comes along

I spoke to you in cautious tones
You answered me with no pretense
And still I feel I've said too much
My silence is my self defense
And every time I've held a rose
Cause when I reach to hold
It seems I've only felt the thorns
And so it goes, and so it goes
And so will you even, I suppose

So you're too young and I'm too old
And New York City's much too cold
And I'm too

But if my silence made you leave
Then that would be my worst mistake
So I will share my room with you
And you can have this heart to break

So you're too young and I'm too old
And I'm so short and you so tall
And New York City's much too cold
And this is showbiz, after all

AND SO IT GOES

Words and Music by
BILLY JOEL

Slow Ballad, with much rubato

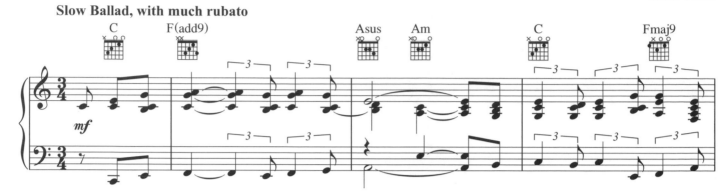

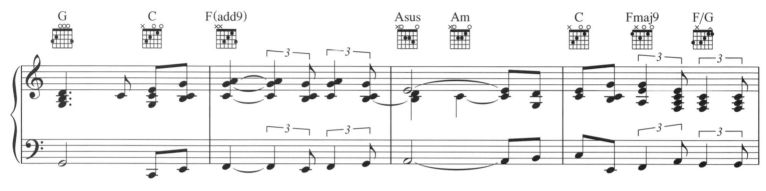

In ev-'ry heart ___ there is a room, a sanc-tu-ar-y safe and
you ___ in cau-tious tones; you an-swered me with no pre-

strong, ___ to heal the wounds ___ from lov-ers past, un-til a new one comes a-
tense. ___ And still I feel ___ I said too much. My si-lence is my self de-

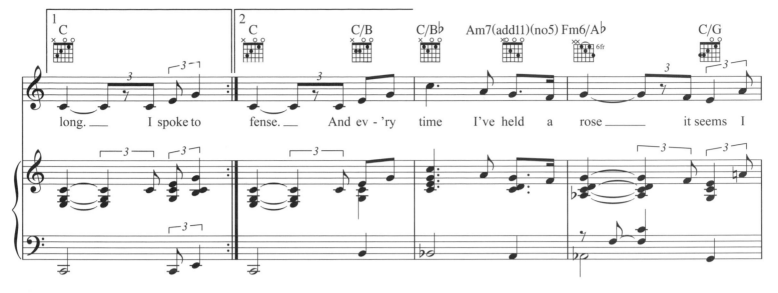

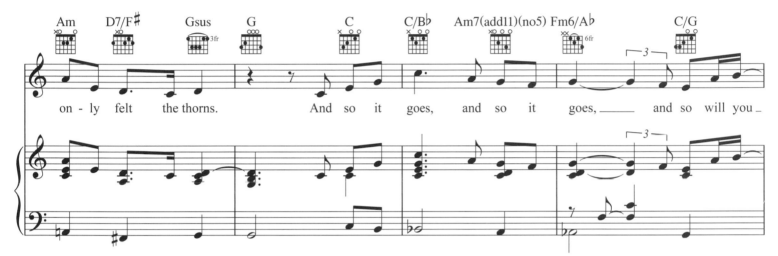

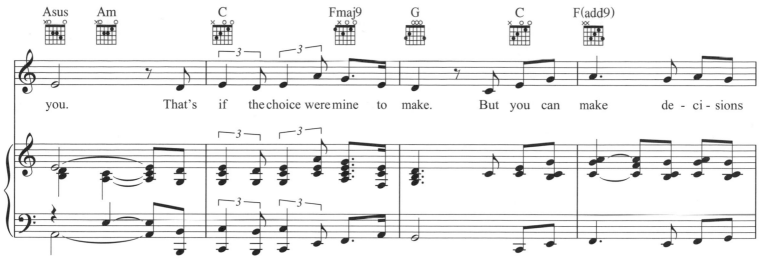

you. That's if the choice were mine to make. But you can make de-ci-sions

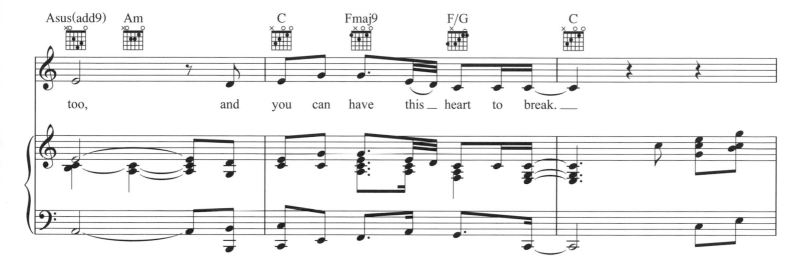

too, and you can have this— heart to break.—

F(add9) Asus Am C Fmaj9 G C

And so it

goes, and so it goes, and you're the on-ly— one who knows.—